Eff You.

Shay Stinson

BookLeaf Publishing

India | USA | UK

Presentation by *BookLeaf Publishing*

Web: www.bookleafpub.com

E-mail: info@bookleafpub.com

ISBN: 9789363309944

First edition 2024

Sometimes I wonder if you're just crazy or
seriously seriously insecure
You ever take a step back and look at yourself in
the mirror?
Pick your self apart the way you do me?
I'm brown
You're not
I'm younger
You're not
I got myself together
You dont
One day I ll be rich
This lifetime, you won't
You so pressed about me
Me pressed about you??
I could never
You so damn stressed about me
Me stressed about you
Hahaha never
You lose sleep over me
I sleep well at night knowing that my life goes
on without you in it
But time and time again you
Wanted me to be the vilian

So here I am

Read on...

2.

"Misery loves company"

The saying goes "misery loves company" and
"mind the company you keep"
Did you think about your consequences when
you put your hands on me?
To wrap those old wrinkled bones around my
neck
Not once
Not twice
Three times
Four times to count
Call me out my name
Degrading me
And never once did I match your energy
You're a coward
Miserable
To think that me walking to your car window
would put an end to your suspicion
You dont want this man but would lay hands on
this goddess
Thinking you would be winning something
You should have choked me harder
Because I like to get fucked up rough
Push me up against your car

Toss my body around the parking lot
Verbally insult me
Like justice would not be on my side
For you to play the little boy who cries wolf
Over and over
Phone call
After
Phone call
To make your self look like the victim
I'm no fool
To be the company in your misery
You play your self
Every time you come after

3.

"Yall be so worried about an image, clean up your Spirit" - msericadixon

Ten plus years being a part of this dysfunctional family. And after Ten plus years and a baby I find out how you really feel about me. I'm a whore, I'm an unfit mother, my family is scum. I'm a n*gger. You prance around as if you are holier than thou, as if there's no skeletons in your closet. Didn't you try to go after your step sister's ex husband? Didn't you accuse your own daughter of sleeping with your ex? Didn't you attack a minor at the family church? Didn't you use your son's second baby mama as a personal live in babysitter? Didn't you shoplift to have dog food?
Didn't you get your house serviced and remodeled illegally? Didn't you use your mother for money to support you on these vacations that you just have to go on because your mom is elderly and needs your support because you think she's incompetent to care for her own self at her own damn vacation with her much earned time share? Uhhh..

Didn't you have a hand in keeping another
woman from her child? And having an ex that
you didn't want pay for your sons legal fees
because you were too selfish to touch money
from your own divorce settlement and family
inheritance?
Didn't you run after that ex husband that left you
and started a whole new family? Oh wait, you
didn't r-u-n after h-i-m you went after his new
woman! Didn't you pressure your mother into
pursuing legal action towards your adopted
brother? Something she didn't want to do..
And this is where it gets good...
Didn't you use what your learned at court to hide
out from getting served restraining order
documents from attacking me? Didn't you crash
your car after speeding away after attacking me?
Didn't you get a new car just so you can stalk
me? Stalk him? Stalk our whole life that doesn't
concern you. Talking all that shit about me but
never taking a look at your self. Mirror mirror
on the wall whose the most conniving,
condescending, raggedy ole haggard of them all?
About face...
Masacarade
Make them all think it's me
When it's you

You raised a stripper who is a gangsta with a
blackass baby daddy, not married but all the
children biracial
But I'm an unfit mother
But I'm a n*gger
You raised a daughter who runs your house
bringing in ever person she was seeing around
her child
But I'm an unfit mother
But I'm a n*gger
You raised a son who fucks his exes gets them
pregnant lies about abuse allegations that your
old boy toy helped finance lawyer fees
But I'm an unfit mother
But I'm a n*gger
You milk the system for workers comp falsifying
disabilities
But out here putting your hands on people
But im an unfit mother
But I'm a n*gger

You have such an evil spirit I wonder how your
demons all get along with each other.

4.

"There are plenty of people who want what you
have or they can live your life better than you
can"- goddess.effect

Better than me?

You try so fucking hard to be.

You may not like that I am the mother of your
brother's child even though him and I broke up
years ago. You try to out do me every chance
that you get. When it comes to my child
M Y C H I L D
M Y D A U G H T E R
You mam, you're just her
A U N T
Nothing more
Buy her clothes, she wears it
Do her hair, she likes it
Get her toys, she plays with it
Take her out, she enjoys it
But you will never
Could ever
Be her M O T H E R.
Mother

I am that
Her Mother
I am that
His ex
I am that
Your ex with me
Oh well, it is that.

Everything I am, bitch you could never be.

5.

"Bitches be pressed. Who the fuck she gon'
check. She be talking that shit, talking out of her
neck."- cardi b press

You hate me so much because of a man you
didn't want and somewhere in this time and
space the universe brought us together way after
you two broke up. What's it to you whether he is
with me or not? He isn't with you, anymore. You
lose sleep over me and I'm not even thinking
about you. Why? Has it ever occurred to you
that you are a none factor in my existence on
this planet? I walk humbly on this earth minding
my own business. You're so pressed about me.
When I don't give a penny for a thought about
you. You're toxic and if I got high you would
blow it. You have distorted characteristics that
my soul does not fuck with. Jealousy is an ugly
trait on you and you're so insecure. Worried
about everything I stand for- me living-- me
breathing-- me being with him--
Shows it. You try to watch what I do, like why
does it matter. Everything that glitters ain't gold,
but bitch I glamour. And you hate it. Again, why
do I matter-- to you? I don't pay your bills, I'm

rent free in your mind. Living my life, I guess you can take note. I can teach you how to flip a coin and preach how to not give an absolute fuck.

6.

"Girl, nobody listen to you 'less you talkin' 'bout me "- cardi b

You act like you're Jesus sitting at the last supper with the twelve apostles gossiping about me. "Maybe she seduced him while we were sleeping." Catty chattering that result in petty arguments. I pity the fool who continues to aim at me as a target. I didn't wreck a home, you threw him out of it. You find everything to turn me into the vilian, presenting your evidence at the table while you and the family sip tea, and i middle finger you all because the jokes will never be on me. Nobody in your family cares to talk to you about real life things like how your injury is fading but you're still faking it. How your ex husband left you the house in settlement and a mortgage you still can't fully pay yet. How you showboat to your neighborhood trying to throw the biggest events, I'm a loser and a freeloader but you're the biggest hypocrite. Every one tunes in to the news broadcast where you report to them how I ruined your life. You make me so relevant you deserve a medal, a standing ovation for giving a speech like a

valedictorian. Does your mouth ever get tired of
speaking me into existence into your painful
lonely boring ole life? You should've had this
much commitment when you were a house wife.
The fuck yous I get and the boohooes you cry,
no body cares to listen unless you call with made
up lies. Me me me and me me me and me me me
again and again. Monday through sunday I'm the
topic of discussion, does talking about me ever
get boring? Because hearing that you all are still
talking about little ole me is absolutely pathetic.

7.

Disrespectfully...

I don't give a f u c k about you being hurt or disrespected about me dating your ex. You will not get an apology. This, I do not regret. I do not care how you feel about me. I do not care about the whole family sided with you and turned their backs on me. I don't give a fuck about the past what you and him did. If you wanted him you would have him and if he wanted he would be there. I don't give a fuck about how he treated you, it ain't me. And since you give way too many fucks about me, you can stay bitter. Stay hating, keep me on your mind.

8.

"A life that isn't yours shouldn't bother you"-
janissa swtstgirl

We are building a life together and you're
bothered. You're pissed off because your brother,
the father of my child broke up. What does that
have to do with you, nothing. That's right
nothing to do with you but you want my life to
be yours, the man, the child, the job, the glory.
He's with me, he loves on me and my child and
you can't stand it, but you sure do watch. You
keep tabs. You keep record. You keep
conversations going about us. But this life of
mine, with him, with us shouldn't bother you.
Then why do you give a fuck about it so much?
We are not your business, but you deserve an
Oscar for theatrics.

Thank you for creating a spectacle out of my
life, continue to view the show. Don't ease up on
the antics.

9.

"Sometimes people hate you because of the way other people love you"- unknown

When you left him, he died. You will never have the old version of him again. You hate the way he loves me. You hate I have his back. You hate the family we have with my daughter. You hate that you care so much about a life that doesn't concern you. You hate me so much like what does my relationships have to do with you? Why are you stressed over a man you treated like shit. He comforted your insecurities in your loneliness and you kept him addicted to his demons. The fact that you fight me over a man you are no longer with, but you don't want, it's obsessive-- the measurements you take to prove one thing: you despise that he's with me. Billions of women in this world and you hate it's me. He can be with whomever he chooses but you hate it's me. You didn't love him properly, you kept him broken. Now that he's healing, watch me love him all the way open. Your mind convinces you it's just sex, he was high, it's money, it's all lies. You want the world to drag me because that's all you want to do. You hate

me because he loves me, he was never meant to
stay with you.

10.

You showed no mercy when you deliberately
drove to my place of residence with an ulterior
motive
--
Thinking you could beat my ass in to leaving
him.
I ruined nothing,
I caused nothing.
Have mercy on you?
Because even prayer I wouldn't say on you.
Spare your feelings?
What feelings do you have?
You should have hit me deeper so you could
leave bruises of me on your knuckles.
Your fist with a blow of hatred to my head.
Yeah, I peeped stone cold eyes
Heart of a dead
Spirit.
You're calculated.
You're spiteful.
Nothing to me.
You mean no well
I won't wish a Nothing
Just a cold day in hell
Upon you.

You reap what you sow
And I ll be watching your karma
With a smirk of gratitude.

Mercy could never be spared upon you, but
I will be
Vindicated.

11.

"They want you madd, bitter and upset. I'm sorry baby God been good to me." - justinlaboy

Everything comes ten fold and I am not wasting my time or energy on haters, enemies, or people who clearly don't like me... YOU. It's a disservice to my self to be mad, to be bitter, to remain upset. I deserve to live my best life as karma knocks at your door. I'm flourishing and you are just getting old.

12.

" I raised the price of access to me... Then I aligned with people who could afford it."- Roberta Tabb

6 months of a restraining order kept you out of my life and away from me. And I will continue to keep you away, from me. You don't deserve access to me. I can't afford to pay out ass whoopings for checks you know you can't cash. You're simply not worth anything so save your last breath.

13.

"Drama at this age is embarrassing. Go find peace and get some money." -Roberta Tabb

You want this man locked up just so he is away from me. You have no barring on our lives but you want to remain relevant. Lurking, spying, trying to dig up dirt. Asking other peoples opinions, trying to get information like you are an investigator building a case, and you wonder why you're hurt. You're in your 60s being childish like a kid, I never knew an old ass woman could be this intoxicated about us like this. You don't work, but you clock in to see what's going on on our side of town. Minding business that don't pay you but you're stressing overtime. I almost feel sorry for you, that you need to create drama to feel important. If you have a heart attack just know you deserved it.

You do this to your self.

14.

"People will literally put you through hell and then act like you're the problem because of how you react to what they have done to you."
-unknown

Point the blame at me for setting up boundaries. You can't hurt me. You caused hell literally on wheels. You raised your arms at my neck, at my face and think I am to bow down and take it. Tell what you want. To whomever you want. They believe what they want. Damage cannot be undone. I'm the problem because I choose to keep you out of my life, then so be it.

15.

"Some people will believe what they want to
believe. As long as you are not hurting anybody,
you don't need to explain yourself. The truth in
your heart matters more than what others think
of you." -Christle/ bloominwithchristle

I owe you
NOTHING.

yes I fucked your ex, he put a ring on it, we live
together with mine and your brother's child and
guess what...

I owe you
NOTHING.

yes you feel I have no morals and I still don't
like you but you continue to taunt me and guess
what...

I owe you
NOTHING.

yes we don't have a restraining order and I still
don't want your crazy ass in my presence or
around my daughter and guess what...

I owe you
NOTHING.

yes this chapter of my life is closed and I will
gracefully bow out of yours even though you
crave the thrill of assaulting me and guess
what...

I still and always will
owe you
NOTHING.

Fuck you and the truth you continue to lie on.

16.

" you are too full of life to let someone's lack of accountability make you feel responsible for their mistakes."- Case Kenny

You coming after me not once but twice was not a mistake. You premeditated assaulting me and then you played victim. I didn't touch you back because why would I jeopardize all that I have built. Your hatred an animosity towards me proves that you are way beneath me. You desperately needed your family to be on your side, it's okay because none of you take accountability for being fucked up spiteful individuals. Pillow talking about how disrespectful I am, your ex is an ex for a reason. It's not like I fucked your man when he was your man. It's seriously hilarious that you 60 year olds are threatened by 30ish me, like I can come in and steal the damn sidewalk and dirt underneath your damn feet.

Where was I wrong?
And you being wrong right?
How do I look my self in the mirror?
--you asked

The same way I fuck your ex every night.

17.

"A person's true colors come out when you
finally hold them accountable for their actions."
-Case Kenny

I got it to where you have limited access to me
and to my child
You may think you have won
But I know way better
You think your vendetta will have me crying in a
corner
You're the only ghost who will be watching over
your shoulder
Sneak disses I can care-less
Yall can kiss my ass from the front and
Straight back
You're delusional to think
I owe you space, time and a thought
Of a bum ass apology
You'll never be with him,
You'll never get next to me
Hate me for protecting my peace
You're a snake
No, I am not sorry
You will never get to share space with me ever
again

Continue to plot and scheme in the background
You'll be watching my life move forward and
blossom
While you up from the ground
I did the court shit and I ll do it again if I have to
I'm always up for war
And this book is my biggest fuck you

18.

"Despite the time someone used you as a
temporary fix, here you are still full of love.
That's strength." -Case Kenny

You used me as a punching bag because you
could not get your way. Vegence is mine now,
you will watch my blessings from the sideline. I
need no get back, no tussle, no fight. I'm still
loved, making money, and will be alright. I'll
never fight over a man but I will stand on
business. Your loss, and I will always have
success. It's not a flex that you believe abusing
me would make you powerful. You still don't
have the man. You're fucking pitiful.

19.

"How do you hate me if I'm on your mind"
-Megan thee stallion

It all started when you assaulted me. We can't
part ways amicably because i run laps in that
mentality disturbing thing you call your brain.
You created a slam campaign to your family. To
slaughter my character and make me a mockery.
How do you hate me 24 7 but if I'm on your
mind, it's because you want me to be. You want
me to be the vilian in your fantasy, but it's you.

You will be your greatest downfall and your
greatest enemy.

20.

32

"I don't give a fuck about you or anything that
you do." - Big Sean

Dear n.e.g.a.t.i.v.e n.a.n.c.y

I am reclaiming all of my peace and I call back
all of my power and my energy.

And disrespectfully,

Fuck you

The end.